THE LITTLE BLACK BOOK OF
GIN
COCKTAILS

First published in Great Britain in 2019 by Pyramid,
an imprint of Octopus Publishing Group Ltd
Carmelite House, 50 Victoria Embankment, London EC4Y 0DZ
www.octopusbooks.co.uk

Distributed in the US by
Hachette Book Group
1290 Avenue of the Americas
4th and 5th Floors
New York, NY 10104

Distributed in Canada by
Canadian Manda Group
664 Annette St.
Toronto, Ontario, Canada M6S 2C8

ISBN 978-0-7537-3368-4

A CIP catalogue record for this book is available from the British Library

Printed and bound in China

10 9 8 7 6 5 4 3 2 1

Publisher: Lucy Pessell
Designer: Lisa Layton
Editor: Sarah Vaughan
Assistant Production Manager: Lucy Carter

The measure that has been used in the recipes is based on a bar jigger, which is 25 ml (1 fl oz).
If preferred, a different volume can be used, providing the proportions are kept constant within
a drink and suitable adjustments are made to spoon measurements, where they occur.

Standard level spoon measurements are used in all recipes.
1 tablespoon = one 15 ml spoon
1 teaspoon = one 5 ml spoon

This book contains cocktails made with raw or lightly cooked eggs. It is prudent for more vulnerable people
to avoid uncooked or lightly cooked cocktails made with eggs.

Some of this material previously appeared in *Hamlyn All Colour Cookery: 200 Classic Cocktails* and *501
Must-Drink Cocktails*.

THE LITTLE BLACK BOOK OF

GIN

COCKTAILS

INTRODUCTION

There are hundreds and hundreds of different cocktails, but there are classics such as the deliciously dry Martini and the lip-smacking Corpse Reviver, or the refreshing Tom Collins and the velvety Negroni that have one luscious ingredient in common: gin.

Here, in *The Little Black Book of Gin Cocktails*, you'll find all the 'ginspiration' you need to recreate all of your favourite classic and contemporary gin cocktails at home.

CONTENTS

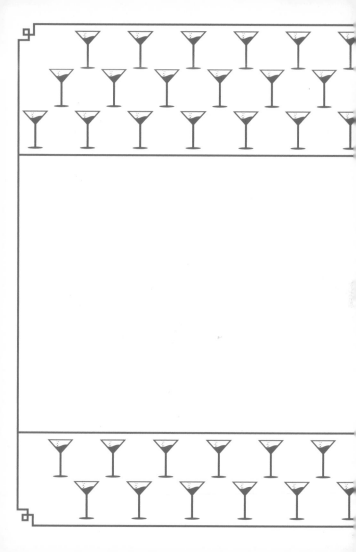

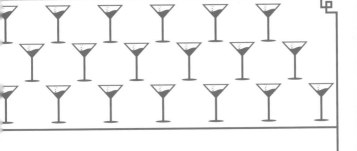

FIZZES,
HIGHBALLS AND
COLLINSES

GIN CUCUMBER COOLER

2 measures gin

5 mint leaves

5 slices cucumber

3 measures apple juice

3 measures soda water

mint sprig, to garnish

Add the gin, mint and cucumber to a glass and gently muddle.

Leave to stand for a couple of minutes, then add the apple juice, soda water and some ice cubes.

Garnish with a mint sprig.

GINTY COLLINS

2 measures gin
1 Earl Grey tea bag
1 measure lemon juice
1 measure sugar syrup
2 teaspoons grapefruit liqueur
2 dashes grapefruit bitters
grapefruit twist, to garnish

Pour the gin into a collins glass and add the Earl Grey tea bag. Allow to steep for 1 minute before removing the tea bag.

Fill a glass with ice cubes and add the lemon juice, sugar syrup, grapefruit liqueur and grapefruit bitters and stir gently.

Garnish with a grapefruit twist and serve.

EDEN'S CLUB COLLINS

2 measures cucumber-infused gin

2 teaspoons elderflower liqueur

5 mint leaves

2 teaspoons lemon juice

2 measures apple juice

3 measures soda water

to garnish:

apple slice (optional)

mint sprig (optional)

Add the cucumber-infused gin, elderflower liqueur, mint leaves, lemon juice and apple juice to a cocktail shaker.

Shake and strain into an ice-filled sling glass.

Top up with 3 measures soda water, garnish with an apple slice or mint sprig and serve.

BERRY COLLINS

makes 2

8 raspberries plus extra,
to garnish
8 blueberries plus extra,
to garnish
1–2 dashes strawberry syrup
4 measures gin
4 teaspoons lemon juice
sugar syrup, to taste
soda water, to top up
lemon slices, to garnish

Muddle the berries and strawberry syrup in the bottom of each glass, then fill each glass with crushed ice.

Add the gin, lemon juice and sugar syrup. Stir, then top up with the soda water.

Garnish with berries and lemon slices and serve.

GINNY GIN FIZZ

2 measures gin

1 camomile tea bag

1 measure sugar syrup

1 measure lemon juice

3 teaspoons egg white

3 measures soda water

lemon twist, to garnish

Place the gin and camomile tea bag in a cocktail shaker and leave to infuse for 2 minutes. Remove the tea bag, add the sugar syrup, lemon juice and egg white.

Fill the shaker with ice cubes. Shake and strain into a wine glass filled with ice cubes and top up with the soda water.

Garnish with a lemon twist and serve.

GIN SLING

makes 2

6 measures gin

2 measures cherry
brandy

juice 1 lemon

soda water, to top up

Add the gin, cherry brandy,
lemon juice and plenty of ice
to a cocktail shaker.

Shake and strain into
2 highball glasses filled with
ice cubes and top up with
soda water.

CITRUS HIGHBALL

1 measure gin
1 citrus tea bag
4 measures low-calorie tonic water
lime or orange wedge, to garnish

Place the gin and citrus tea bag in a collins glass and leave to infuse for 2 minutes.

Remove the tea bag, fill the glass with ice cubes and top up with low-calorie tonic water.

Stir, then garnish with a lime or orange wedge and serve.

17

CAMOMILE COLLINS

2 measures gin
1 camomile tea bag
1 measure lemon juice
1 measure sugar syrup
4 measures soda water
lemon slice, to garnish

Pour the gin into a glass and add the tea bag.

Stir the tea bag and gin together, for about 5 minutes, until the gin is infused with the camomile flavour.

Remove the tea bag and fill the glass with ice cubes.

Add the remaining ingredients and garnish with a lemon slice.

RIVIERA
FIZZ

makes 2

3 measures sloe gin

1 measure lemon juice

1 measure sugar syrup

Champagne, chilled, to
top up

lemon twists, to garnish

Put the sloe gin, lemon
juice and sugar syrup into
a cocktail shaker and add
some ice cubes.

Shake and strain into
2 chilled flutes.

Top up with Champagne,
stir, garnish each with a
lemon twist and serve.

STRAWBERRY FIELDS

2 measures gin

1 camomile tea bag

1 measure strawberry purée

1 measure double cream

3 teaspoons egg white

4 measures soda water, chilled

strawberry, to garnish

Place the gin and the camomile tea bag in a cocktail shaker and leave to infuse for 2 minutes.

Remove the tea bag and then add the strawberry purée, lemon juice, double cream and egg white to the shaker.

Shake and strain into a wine glass and top up with 4 measures chilled soda water. Garnish with a strawberry and serve.

ROYAL COBBLER

3 teaspoons gin

3 teaspoons fino sherry

3 teaspoons raspberry and pineapple syrup

2 teaspoons lemon juice

3 measures Prosecco, chilled

raspberry, to garnish (optional)

orange twist, to garnish (optional)

Add the gin, fino sherry, raspberry and pineapple syrup and lemon juice to a cocktail shaker.

Shake and strain into a flute glass and top up with the chilled Prosecco.

Garnish with a raspberry or orange twist and serve.

FRENCH AFTERNOON

1 measure gin

3 teaspoons camomile tea syrup

2 dashes peach bitters

4 measures Champagne, chilled

lemon twist, to garnish

Add the gin, camomile tea syrup, lemon juice and peach bitters to a cocktail shaker.

Shake and strain into a flute glass, top up with the chilled Champagne and garnish with a lemon twist.

ORCHARD COLLINS

1 measure gin

3 teaspoons lemon juice

3 teaspoons camomile and fennel seed shrub

1 measure apple juice

4 measures cider

apple slice, to garnish

Add the gin, lemon juice, camomile and fennel seed shrub and apple juice to a cocktail shaker and shake.

Strain into a collins glass filled with ice cubes and top up with the cider.

Garnish with an apple slice and serve.

FINO HIGHBALL

4 clementine slices

2 lemon slices

1 measure gin

1 measure fino sherry

2 teaspoons passion fruit syrup

2 measures low-calorie tonic water

lemon wedge, to garnish

Muddle the clementine and lemon slices in a cocktail shaker and then add the gin, fino sherry and passion fruit syrup.

Fill cocktail shaker with ice cubes. Shake, then strain into a glass.

Add the tonic water and fill the glass with crushed ice.

Garnish with a lemon wedge and serve.

MANGO RICKY

5 basil leaves plus extra, to garnish
2 lime wedges
1 measure mango-infused gin
2 teaspoons sugar syrup
2 measures soda water

Roughly tear the basil leaves and add to a glass.

Squeeze the lime wedges into the glass and then add them to the glass.

Add the gin, sugar syrup and soda water, then top up the glass with crushed ice.

Garnish with basil leaves and serve.

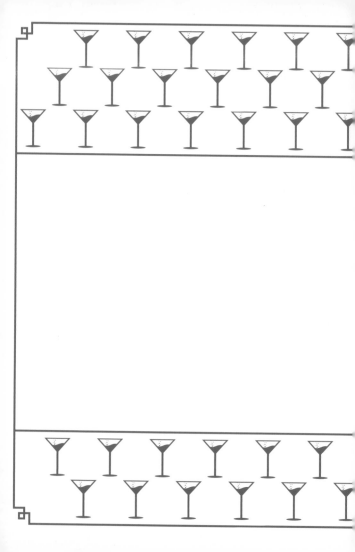

SPIRIT
FORWARDS

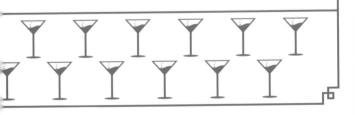

MARTINEZ

2 measures gin
3 teaspoons sweet vermouth
2 teaspoons orange liqueur
2 dashes Angostura bitters
orange twist, to garnish

Fill a glass with ice cubes and add all the ingredients.

Stir, garnish with an orange twist and serve.

SMOKY MARTINI

makes 2

½ measure dry vermouth

4 measures gin

2 measures sloe gin

10 drops orange bitters

orange twists, to garnish

Put some ice cubes into a mixing glass, add ½ measure dry vermouth and stir until the ice cubes are well coated.

Pour in the gins then add the orange bitters. Stir well, then strain into 2 chilled cocktail glasses and add an orange twist to each.

MAIDEN'S PRAYER

makes 2

4 measures gin

4 measures Cointreau

2 measures orange juice

Pour the gin into a cocktail shaker with some ice cubes. Add the Cointreau and orange juice.

Shake well, then strain into 2 chilled Martini glasses to serve.

MOON RIVER

makes 2

1 measure dry gin
1 measure apricot brandy
1 measure Cointreau
½ measure Galliano
½ measure lemon juice
maraschino cherries, to garnish

Put some ice cubes into a cocktail shaker. Pour the gin, apricot brandy, Cointreau, Galliano and lemon juice over the ice.

Shake then strain into 2 large chilled Martini glasses.

Garnish each with a cherry.

FRENCH PINK LADY

2 measures gin
1 measure triple sec
4 raspberries
3 teaspoons lime juice
1 teaspoon pastis
lime wedge, to garnish

Add the gin, triple sec, raspberries, lime juice and pastis to a cocktail shaker and muddle.

Fill the shaker with ice cubes and shake, then strain into a glass.

Garnish with a lime wedge and serve.

TIPPERARY

3 measures gin
3 measures dry vermouth
juice 1 lemon

Add all the ingredients, including some ice cubes, into a mixing glass.

Stir gently and strain into a chilled cocktail glass.

FAIR LADY

lightly beaten egg white
caster sugar
1 measure gin
1 dash Cointreau
4 measures grapefruit juice

Frost the rim of an old-fashioned glass by dipping it into egg white and pressing it into the sugar.

Add the remaining ingredients, including the remaining egg white and some ice cubes, into a cocktail shaker.

Shake well, then pour into the prepared glass.

RED RUM

makes 2

1 measure sloe gin

handful of redcurrants
plus extra, to garnish

4 measures Bacardi
8-year-old rum

1 measure lemon juice

1 measure vanilla syrup

Muddle the sloe gin and
redcurrants together in
a cocktail shaker.

Add the rum, lemon juice,
vanilla syrup and some
ice cubes.

Shake and double-strain
into 2 chilled Martini
glasses, garnish with
redcurrants and serve.

BITTERSWEET SYMPHONY

1 measure gin
1 measure Campari
½ measure passion fruit syrup
½ measure lemon juice
lemon slices, to garnish

Put some ice cubes into a cocktail shaker with all the ingredients and shake to mix.

Strain into an old-fashioned glass over 4–6 ice cubes and garnish with lemon slices.

ZED

1 measure gin

1 measure Mandarine Napoléon brandy

3 measures pineapple juice

1 teaspoon sugar

to garnish:

half lemon slices

mint sprig

pineapple wedge

orange rind strips

Put some cracked ice into a cocktail shaker and pour the gin, Mandarine Napoléon brandy, pineapple juice and sugar over it.

Shake lightly to mix and pour into a tall glass.

Garnish with half lemon slices, a mint sprig, a pineapple wedge and orange rind strips.

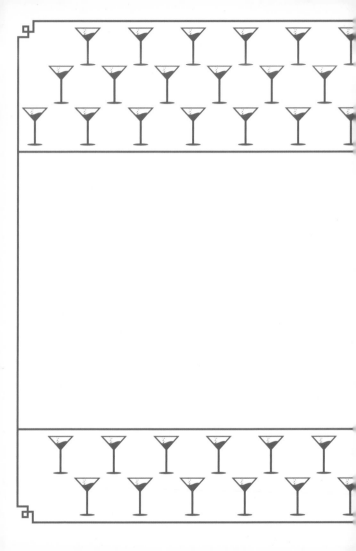

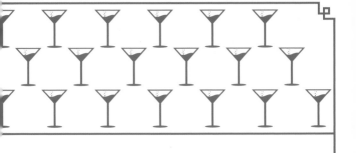

SOURS

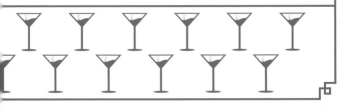

KIWI SMASH

½ kiwi fruit, quartered, plus an extra slice, to garnish

4 slices lemon

4 teaspoons sugar syrup

2 measures gin

1 coriander sprig

Add the kiwi fruit, lemon and sugar syrup to a glass and muddle. Add the gin and coriander and half-fill the glass with crushed ice.

Churn with the muddler until thoroughly mixed. Top up with more crushed ice, garnish with a kiwi fruit slice and serve.

SOUTHSIDE ROYALE

2 measures gin
4 slices cucumber
3 teaspoons lime juice
3 teaspoons sugar syrup
4 mint leaves plus extra,
to garnish
1 measure Prosecco,
chilled

Add the gin, cucumber, lime juice, sugar syrup, mint leaves and ice cubes to a cocktail shaker. Shake and strain into a Martini glass.

Top up with 1 measure chilled Prosecco, garnish with mint leaf and serve.

GREEN BAY COLADA

2 measures gin

½ kiwi fruit, quartered, plus an extra slice, to garnish

4 cubes, about 5 cm (2 inches) each, cantaloupe melon

1 teaspoon ginger juice

2 teaspoons lemon juice

1 measure agave syrup

1 coriander sprig

Add the gin, kiwi fruit, cantaloupe melon, ginger juice, lemon juice, agave syrup, coriander and 1 cup ice cubes to a food processor or blender. Blend until smooth.

Pour into a sling glass, garnish with a kiwi slice and serve.

BETSY

makes 2

2 measures gin
4 teaspoons lime juice
1 measure sugar syrup
2 strawberries plus
extra, to garnish
1 coriander sprig

Add all the ingredients plus
1 cup ice cubes to a food
processor or blender and
blend until smooth.

Pour into 2 glasses, garnish
each with a half a strawberry
and serve.

WEST SIDE PINK FLAMINGO

makes 2

100 ml (3½ fl oz) gin
1 measure lime juice
1 measure strawberry syrup
2 measures strawberry purée
250 ml (8 fl oz) rosé wine
250 ml (8 fl oz) watermelon juice
2 mint sprigs plus extra, to garnish

Add all the ingredients to a food processor or blender and give it short blitzes to coarsely chop the mint.

Pour into a shallow freezer container and freeze for 24 hours.

Remove from the freezer and stir with a fork to create a granita.

Spoon into 2 wine glasses, garnish each with a mint sprig and serve with a spoon.

HONG KONG SLING

½ measure gin

½ measure lychee liqueur

1 measure lychee purée

1 measure lemon juice

½ measure sugar syrup

soda water, to top up

fresh lychee in its shell, to garnish

Add all the ingredients except the soda water to a cocktail shaker and shake and strain into a sling glass.

Top up with soda water, garnish with a lychee and serve with long straws.

GIN GARDEN MARTINI

makes 2

½ cucumber, peeled and chopped, plus extra slices, to garnish

1 measure elderflower cordial

4 measures gin

2 measures pressed apple juice

Muddle the cucumber in the bottom of a cocktail shaker with the elderflower cordial.

Add the gin, apple juice and some ice cubes.

Shake and double-strain into 2 chilled Martini glasses, garnish with peeled cucumber slices and serve.

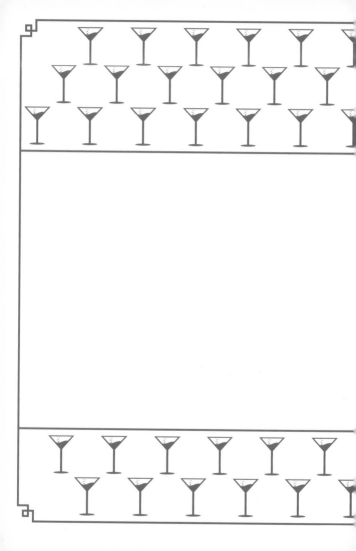

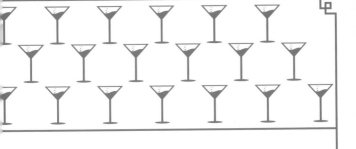

SHARERS
AND
PUNCHES

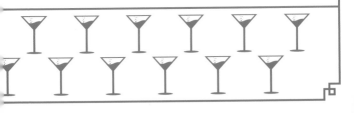

PIMM'S COCKTAIL

makes 2

2 measures Pimm's
No. 1 Cup

2 measures gin

4 measures lemonade

4 measures ginger ale

to garnish:
cucumber strips
blueberries
orange slices

Fill 2 highball glasses with
ice cubes. Add all the
ingredients, one by one in
order, over the ice.

Garnish with cucumber strips,
blueberries and orange slices
and serve.

GINGER LANGRA

makes 1 large jug

4 measures ginger and green cardamon-infused gin

4 measures fino sherry

2 measures mango juice

2 measures lemon juice

2 measures sugar syrup

200 ml (7 fl oz) tonic water

lime wheels, to garnish

Add the gin, fino sherry, mango juice, lemon juice, sugar syrup and tonic water to a large jug full of ice cubes and stir.

Garnish with lime wheels and serve.

SYLVESTRE PUNCH

makes 1 large jug

4 measures gin
1 tablespoon marmalade
1 measure lemon juice
4 measures orange juice
4 measures pink grapefruit juice
250 ml (8 fl oz) Earl Grey tea, chilled
6 measures mineral water

Place all the ingredients in a food processor or blender and blend until smooth. Place in a soda syphon and charge with carbon dioxide, following the manufacturer's instructions.

Chill in the refrigerator for at least 1 hour in the soda syphon.

Pour into a large serving jug to serve.

LANGRA
AND TONIC

makes 1 large jug

200 ml (7 fl oz) gin
4 measures mango juice
2 measures lemon juice
2 measures sugar
200 ml (7 fl oz) tonic water
lemon wheels, to garnish

Fill a jug with ice cubes, add all the ingredients and stir.

Garnish with lemon wheels and serve.

EARL'S PUNCH

makes 1 large jug

4 measures gin

6 measures Earl Grey tea, chilled

6 measures pink grapefruit juice

6 measures soda water

1 measure sugar syrup

to garnish:
pink grapefruit slices
black cherries

Fill a jug with ice cubes. Add all the remaining ingredients and stir.

Garnish with pink grapefruit slices and black cherries and serve.

ON THE LAWN

makes 2

strawberries

orange segments, peeled

2 measures gin

2 measures Pimm's
No. 1 Cup

lemonade, to top up

ginger ale, to top up

Fill 2 highball glasses with ice cubes and fresh fruit such as strawberries and peeled orange segments.

Add the gin and Pimm's No. 1 Cup to each glass and top up with lemonade and ginger ale.

HONEYDEW PUNCH

makes 1 large jug

3 measures gin

1 measure strawberry liqueur

8 measures honeydew
melon juice

2 measures lime juice

2 measures sugar syrup

1 bunch mint leaves, torn

Prosecco, to top up

to garnish:
honeydew melon slices

strawberries

mint sprigs

Add all the ingredients to a jug
or punch bowl filled with ice
cubes and stir well.

Garnish with slices of honeydew
melon, strawberries and sprigs
of mint.

GARDEN COOLER

makes 1 large punch bowl

700 ml (1¼ pints) London dry gin

500 ml (17 fl oz) lemon juice

250 ml (8 fl oz) sugar syrup

250 ml (8 fl oz) elderflower cordial

500 ml (17 fl oz) green tea, cooled

500 ml (17 fl oz) mint tea, cooled

500 ml (17 fl oz) apple juice

500 ml (17 fl oz) soda water

peach slices, to garnish

Add all the ingredients to a punch bowl filled with ice cubes and stir.

Garnish with peach slices and serve.

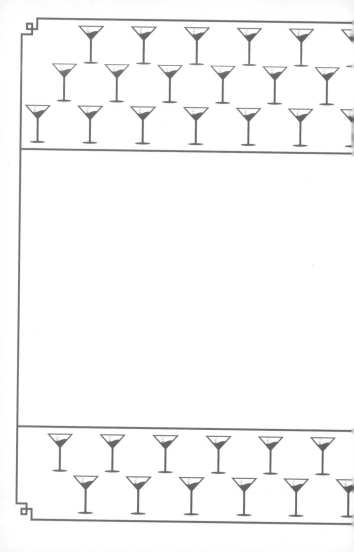

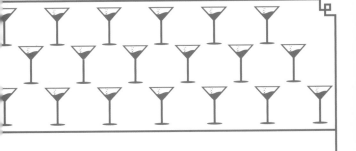

CLASSICS

MARTINI

makes 2

1 measure dry vermouth
6 measures gin
stuffed green olives,
to garnish

Put 10–12 ice cubes into a mixing glass.

Pour over the vermouth and gin and stir (never shake) vigorously and evenly, and without splashing.

Strain into 2 chilled Martini glasses, garnish each with a green olive and serve.

CLOVER CLUB

2 measures gin

¾ measure lemon juice

¾ measure sugar syrup

5 raspberries plus extra, to garnish

½ measure egg white

Add all the ingredients to your cocktail shaker and dry shake without ice for 10 seconds.

Take the shaker apart, add some ice cubes and then shake vigorously.

Strain into a cocktail glass and garnish with raspberries.

THE FIX

makes 2

4 measures gin
1 dash lime juice
1 dash lemon juice
1 dash pineapple juice
1 measure Cointreau

Add all the ingredients in a cocktail shaker filled with ice.

Shake and strain into 2 chilled highball glasses.

TOM COLLINS

2 measures gin
1 measure sugar syrup
1 measure lemon juice
4 measures soda water

to garnish:
lemon wedge
black cherry

Put the gin, sugar syrup and lemon juice into a cocktail shaker and fill with ice cubes.

Shake and strain into a glass full of ice cubes and top up with the soda water.

Garnish with a lemon wedge and a cherry.

SINGAPORE SLING

makes 2

2 measures gin
1 measure cherry brandy
½ measure Cointreau
½ measure Bénédictine
1 measure grenadine
1 measure lime juice
10 measures pineapple juice
1–2 dashes Angostura bitters

to garnish:
pineapple wedges
cocktail cherries

Half-fill a cocktail shaker with ice cubes and put some ice cubes into 2 highball glass.

Add all the ingredients to the shaker and shake until a frost forms on the outside of the shaker.

Strain over the ice cubes into the glasses and garnish each with a pineapple wedge and a cocktail cherry to serve.

GIMLET

2½ measures gin
½ measure lime cordial
½ measure lime juice
lime rind spiral, to garnish

Add all the ingredients to a cocktail shaker. Shake and strain into a chilled cocktail glass.

Garnish with a lime rind spiral.

MONKEY GLAND

1 measure orange juice
2 measures gin
3 dashes pernod
3 dashes grenadine

Put 3–4 ice cubes into a cocktail shaker with all the ingredients.

Shake well, then strain into a chilled cocktail glass.

FRENCH 75

makes 2

2 measures gin
6 teaspoons lemon juice
6 teaspoons sugar syrup
8 measures Champagne, chilled
lemon twist, to garnish

Add the gin, lemon juice and sugar syrup into a cocktail shaker and shake.

Strain into 2 flute glasses and top up with the chilled Champagne.

Garnish with a lemon twist and serve.

LONG ISLAND ICED TEA

makes 2

1 measure gin
1 measure vodka
1 measure white rum
1 measure tequila
1 measure Cointreau
1 measure lemon juice
cola, to top up
lemon slices, to garnish

Put the gin, vodka, rum, tequila, Cointreau and lemon juice in a cocktail shaker with some ice cubes and shake to mix.

Strain into 2 highball glasses filled with ice cubes and top up with cola.

Garnish with lemon slices and serve.

AVIATION

2 measures gin

½ measure maraschino liqueur

½ measure lemon juice

cocktail cherry, to garnish

Put some ice cubes into a cocktail shaker with the gin, maraschino liqueur and lemon juice.

Shake well and double strain into a chilled Martini glass.

Garnish with a cocktail cherry on a cocktail stick.

FLORADORA

2 measures gin
½ teaspoon grenadine
juice of ½ lime
½ teaspoon sugar syrup
dry ginger ale, to top up
lime rind twist, to garnish

Put 4–5 ice cubes into a cocktail shaker, add all the ingredients, apart from the ginger ale, and shake until a frost forms on the outside of the shaker.

Pour without straining into a hurricane glass, top up with ginger ale and garnish with a lime rind twist.

SOUTHSIDE

2 measures gin

4 teaspoons lime juice

4 teaspoons sugar syrup

5 mint leaves plus extra,
to garnish

Add all the ingredients to a cocktail shaker with some ice cubes.

Shake and strain into a glass. Garnish with a mint leaf and serve.

91

NEGRONI

1 measure gin
1 measure sweet vermouth
1 measure Campari
orange wedges, to garnish

Fill a glass with ice cubes, add all the ingredients and stir.

Garnish with an orange wedge and serve.

PINK GIN

2 measures gin
5 dashes Angostura bitters
still water, to top up

Add all ingredients to an old-fashioned glass filled with ice cubes and stir briefly before serving.

VESPER MARTINI

2½ measures gin
1 measure vodka
½ measure Lillet blanc wine
lemon twist, to garnish

Add all the ingredients into the bottom of a cocktail shaker, and fill the top half of it with ice.

Shake vigorously and double strain into a chilled Martini glass.

Garnish with a lemon twist.

PICTURE
ACKNOWLEDGEMENTS

cover and interior icons:
Noun Project   Okan Benn,
Hermine Blanquart, Arif Fajar
Yulianto, Marco Livolsi

interior images:
Octopus Publishing Group
Stephen Conroy 12, 36, 42, 57, 61,
74, 81, 87; Jonathan Kennedy 9, 15,
18, 23, 26, 29, 33, 39, 49, 52, 64,
67, 70, 78, 84, 90, 93